Conchas y Café Zine

Vol. VI, Issue 3

UNI dos

a DSTL arts publication

DSTL Arts presents

UNIdos

Conchas y Café Zine
Vol. VI, Issue 3

The work in this book was written by participants from DSTL Arts's Conchas y Café creative writing program, and first printed in May, 2021 by DSTL Arts publishing.

Cover and Book Design: Luis Antonio Pichardo

ISBN: 978-1-946081-52-0

10 9 8 7 6 5 4 3 2 1

www.DSTLArts.org

DSTL arts

Los Angeles, CA

Table of Contents

The Poem 1
David Fallon

Feed on My Words 5
Ani Minasian

dream loudly 7
Karyn Grasse

Silence… the Final Frontier 9
Luz Donis

Speak Only to Me 11
Lois Jackson King

Literally 212°F 12
Abraham Jaramillo

the truth about procrastination 13
Mauricio "Soul on Fire" Moreno

If I Told You My Name 14
Gustavo R. Ramirez

A Million and One Fireflies 15
Felicia Taylor E.

Open the Door 17
Kathy Vega

Power Within 18
Lois Jackson King

Part II 19
Michelle Smith

you push/up the moon 21
Karyn Grasse

El Único 23
Luz Donis

Greed 25
Abraham Jaramillo

Hear Me 29
Felicia Taylor E.

Aayo 31
Gustavo R. Ramirez

Lotería 33
Sanjuanita Martinez

Go Forward Please 35
Lois Jackson King

Maybe U Can 36
Mauricio "Soul on Fire" Moreno

stardust 44
Karyn Grasse

Who Am I? 46
Sanjuanita Martinez

I See You 49
Ani Minasian

Layers of a Generation 51
Felicia Taylor E.

Write and Wrong 53
Tina Fallon

My Hands 54
Kathy Vega

Poetic Exploration....56
Ani Minasian

Person....58
Abraham Jaramillo

Seven Stars in Heaven....60
Gustavo R. Ramirez

The Promise....64
Sanjuanita Martinez

Word Food....66
David Fallon

Unity Wheel....69
Kathy Vega

Prophecy Resurrected—Our Rallying Cry....71
Gustavo R. Ramirez

Latest News!....72
Sanjuanita Martinez

Part III....74
Michelle Smith

Sliding....76
Tina Fallon

¡Marcha!....78
Gustavo R. Ramirez

Here to Serve You....83
Kathy Vega

I Feel like a Cog in the Machine/Am I Married to My Job?....85
Michelle Smith

Shoes Could Talk....87
Lois Jackson King

Bricks....88
Tina Fallon

A Simple Walk on The Twilight of the Pandemic.....90
Karyn Grasse

My Beloved Spirit.....92
Kathy Vega

She Has a Cat.....93
David Fallon

The Fruits of Life.....95
Lois Jackson King

Part IV.....96
Michelle Smith

Unify.....97
Gustavo R. Ramirez

Question.....99
Lois Jackson King

The World Needs Love.....100
Sanjuanita Martinez

Your Life Matters.....103
Gustavo R. Ramirez

Love thy Neighbor: Step by Step.....105
Luz Donis

Vibration of the Spirit.....106
Lois Jackson King

Mortified.....107
Tina Fallon

Inspiration Studies.....109
Kathy Vega

A Touch of Heaven.....111
Gustavo R. Ramirez

shot.....112
Karyn Grasse

Hope 113
Lois Jackson King

Mind Archeology 114
Nery Martinez, Jr.

Stop Worrying 117
Lois Jackson King

Delectable Collectables 118
Michelle Smith

Changes 120
Sanjuanita Martinez

Tick-Tock Clock of Life 122
Lois Jackson King

Always No 123
Tina Fallon

Touch Down in Store 125
Lois Jackson King

The Poem

for Nikolai

David Fallon

We picked up a poem at the poem store. It was an impulse buy,
something we never would have considered, but somehow
it spoke to us.

When we brought it home, it was kind of light and airy
like Spring clouds. It hovered pleasantly around the room
and made us feel nice.

As with most things, we eventually got bored of the poem
and stopped looking at it. Months went by and the poem was
all but forgotten.

One night after a late movie and some drinks
at the bar, we came home to find the poem on the couch
eating Doritos and watching Big Bang Theory.

We told it to get off the furniture: furniture is not
where poems belong! It gave us an angry look before slinking
under the dining room table.

It sulked there for a very long time. The tension grew
day by day as we waited for it to leave, to go live

its own life. Anywhere but here.

But my wife started to feel guilty, as she often does.
"We can't just throw the poem out onto the streets."
And of course she was right.

I bought the poem a suit, and got it some job
interviews. It blew every one of them, and started
to make grumbling sounds.

My wife helped the poem enroll in college where it took
some art and cooking classes. When I suggested engineering
you would not believe the look it gave me.

Unfortunately, it could not pass the math classes required
for its degree. It withdrew again, this time behind the refrigerator,
where it rattled the door loudly every time we walked by.

The poem was extremely depressed, so we took it to a therapist
that talked to the poem and did some tests. After a few weeks,
the therapist suggested we try having a conversation with the poem.

We tried to sit and speak with the poem,
but it shrugged and walked away. It settled, unhappy,
into a corner in the back of the house.

Several years later, in our desperation to connect with other people, we invited another couple over for dinner. We had a great time eating brisket and drinking wine.

Our heads and hearts were light from laughter and wine,
so we didn't notice when the lady visitor wandered off
to the back of the house.

Suddenly, we were broken from our revelry as we heard her exclaim loudly, "What is this?!" and ran as if we were trying to get to the scene of a crime.

There was the poem, sleeping in its corner. It had pilfered
one of the bottles of wine and drained it dry until
it passed out in its misery.

Before we could explain or apologize, the lady gasped with
a tear in her eye, "That's the most beautiful poem
I've ever seen!"

My wife and I did a double take. To us the poem was
a terrible eyesore, like something out of place.
What could she possibly see in it?

"Would you like to have it?" my wife simply said. After the obligatory refusal, the lady eventually caved. She left the party with the poem in her arms and a smile on her face.

We thought we would be relieved to finally see the poem gone, but all we felt was emptiness, as if we had just surrendered something of importance.

Feed on My Words

Ani Minasian

Share your harvest with me

I'll sow your fields with poems and painted flowers

Shelter me

I'll lay out for you a feast of stories and gilded songs

I don't need much

I can live on silence and some scraps of paper

I know I can't perform brain surgery or build you a bridge

But I can gather stardust and manufacture dreams

I can invent languages and engineer worlds unseen

And when I construct the museum of your life

Every heartbreak, joy, victory and strife

All your deepest truths will finally ring out

Your untold secrets sung aloud...

Maybe one day

when you're done laying bricks

or reading contracts or meeting with

clients or packing lunches for your kids
or launching a new marketing campaign

maybe then you'll weep
with me and my heart

breathe my soul
and my music

and feed
on my words

dream loudly

Karyn Grasse

it is the holy work of the poet to dream into being the better world.

dream of a better world loudly, clouds lay
at your feet sweetly when you reach
star-ward, rewarding you with gossamer
hope, afloat with ideals. it is real, this appeal
to our better angels. they stoop down
to lift us up, rise up, realize up,
your fellow wo(man) can stand
on your shoulders if your bolder
instincts lift them from the brink. can we think
of a brighter world, swirled around a
thawing love, drawing us into an evolution
of humanity? can a love grown cold
wake? can we take the steps up the mountain and out
of the abyss? YES. there is a higher call, all of us long to
be seen, with a sheen of
dignity, integrity, possibility. grow wings
and fly out of the valley of
shouting, of doubting, mounting up on eagle's
wings as a new dawn sings its

blinding song clear as

truth. you must use it to sing all things

new. it starts with

you.

Silence... the Final Frontier

based on a study published in* Science *July 2014

Luz Donis

In 1654, scientist and philosopher, Blaise Pascal, wrote: "All of humanity's problems stem from man's inability to sit quietly in a room alone and write a poem."

Now, there's some science behind that statement. A recent study in the journal, *Science*, found that many people choose to self-administer an electric shock rather than sit quietly in a room alone with their thoughts and construct a poem.

The study recruited hundreds of undergraduate volunteers and community members to participate in "thinking periods." Individuals were placed in sparsely furnished rooms and asked to put away their belongings, such as cellphones and pens. They took two tests lasting 6-15 minutes. Some were told to think about whatever they wanted, others chose from several prompts. The volunteers then rated their experience, about 50% did not like the experience. The participants gave high ratings of boredom and writer's block.

To see if a change of scenario would help, the team let participants do the studies at their own home, but the results were similar.

The researchers took the experiment a step further. Leaving the participants alone in the lab with their poetic thoughts for 15 minutes. There were only two rules: they could not get out of the chairs, and they couldn't fall asleep. They could push a button and shock themselves if they wanted to. They had tried the shock just for practice, and knew how unpleasant it was. The results were startling. 67% of men and 25% of women chose to inflict themselves rather than just sit quietly and think.

"We went into this thinking it wouldn't be hard for people to entertain themselves. We have this huge brain and it's stuffed full of pleasant memories, and we have the ability to construct fantasies and stories. We really thought this [thinking time] was something people would like," says Timothy Wilson, social psychologist at the University of Virginia. He suggests that the results may be signs of boredom and the trouble we have controlling our thoughts.

Some people seem to enjoy thinking more than others. For instance, writers, self-identifying introverts, and those who admitted that their daydreams normally leave them happy, fared better.

The research suggests that meditation, or other techniques to relax and learn how to gain control of the mind, could be helpful. If we knew how to steer our thoughts in a pleasant direction and enjoy the experience, maybe we wouldn't hate to be alone with ourselves and our poems.

Speak Only to Me

Lois Jackson King

Speak to me now, and tell me what I need to hear while I am
still near

Tell me what you know is true, without any fear

Mouth to speak words of your heart

Let no man drive a wedge to set us apart

Time is short, don't play games; these things refrain from

There is no force field to go through

No hurdle elements to jump through

Satisfying technology that can't be seen

Your power does not need plug-in

Yet source is powering the world

Laboratory-minds blown and mouth open

All that is done equipped by heavenly source

Acceptance of gifts and talent, do the best, and to God leaving
the rest

No list of rules; you don't have to pass a test

Once you say yes, I assure you, you'll have all the best

Literally 212°F

Abraham Jaramillo

Words create the clouds
all the moisture from the seas crowds up
thanks to words the atmosphere exist

words leave our bodies from
every heated pore

deserts need more water, but
words take it away faster
than it can be collected

words kept the steam engines
on the move

words remove the salt and
other impurities of the water

if words didn't exist
this dynamic world
Neither.

the truth about procrastination

Mauricio "Soul on Fire" Moreno

I'm trying to find the words,   but all I find are cobwebs

I'm trying to find cobwebs,   but all I find are words

I'm trying to find,   but words are webs

I'm trying words,   but find webs

I find words,   in webs

In words, I find I

If I Told You My Name

Gustavo R. Ramirez

If I told you my name would you call me God's staff?

If I told you my story would you mock me and laugh?

If I opened my heart would you share in the pain?

Would you scoff? Would you balk and say it's all in vain?

If I told you my story.

If I shared with you deeply would you laugh? Would you cry?

If we shared together

Would we cry till we couldn't deny?

Would we cry till we both dried our eyes?

So let's share our stories, and share them with pride.

The good pride–no boasting. We'll have love on our side.

So let's share together. We will feel. We will see.

Let's finally hug and at last we'll be free.

A Million and One Fireflies

Felicia Taylor E.

I've almost lost you thrice

Falling to my knees of what I thought was the final round

They picked me up, grabbing each arm in that *slow motion dance*

I cannot live without you

Our love has burned as a million and one fireflies

Why have you tried to leave me? You know can't be *we* if you
are gone

I cannot exist with you gone

Butterfly wings you've given hold me up

Angelic motioning from the God of light, Abraham and Moses
infuse us

When your ashes float beyond this realm's eternal core

I will follow you, like a leaf swirling from a branch or twig

My flow with you is from

beginning to end

Open the Door

Kathy Vega

Open the door and let me in so that I can be in the room with you.

You are in the room with the door open waiting to let me in.

Let me in the room with the open door that brings us together.

The open door lets me in to be with you.

You are the open door that allows me in.

Your door is open for me.

I am going in.

Power Within

Lois Jackson King

To design courage

To persuade pride

To convince a sureness

To set to a challenge

To embellish ability

To honor heritage of our roots

To set destinies

To enhance richness

To believe in self

To establish power

To create legacies

To exhort sounding out

To help to stand

To keep the ink-well full

To believe you're not alone

To inspire, to keep hope alive

To show kindness of heart

To bring knowledge of element harvesting to life

To face reality of pro's and con's

To accept differences

To view victory in advance

Part II

Michelle Smith

I am the cog in the asisstive living facility

machine

Robotics have nothing on me

Up and down

Side to side

Transfer from the bed to the wheelchair

Or raised commode

I am a well-oiled machine

And the Tin Man from the *Wizard of Oz* with a heart

There's 15 residents to serve

At times they may grate on your nerves

Individual and similar

Mind, body, spirit, and verve

We workers are busy and lovingly

The nitty gritty

Taking them to bingo or an exercise activity

Yes WD-40 is not the same as *Red, Red Wine* by UB40

My steel and strength can only take so much

My heart, patience, and drive sustains me

And will there be a well oiled machine to care for me

In my silver Tsunami years

Or a Tin Man with a heart?

The future cog in my machine

Encourage me because one day you will be me

And I will be them

you push/up the moon

Karyn Grasse

way maker, grain
harvester, road builder, stomach
filler,
with grizzled ropes you
pull up the sun, the hemp

cuts into your
hands.

water finder, home
maker, word bringer, tunnel
cutter, between clenched teeth

you rip clouds
from the sky.

people mover, light
bringer, can emptier, grave
digger, with bared shoulders you push

up the moon, the sweat
of your brow becomes rain

and we

are

que

nc

he

d.

El Único

Luz Donis

Soy un mono

feo y peludo, en veces

hablo en monosílabas

escucho en estéreo.

Construyo monolitos

corto, conquisto

y monopolizo.

Tiendo ser muy monótono

a pesar que tengo

manos con pulgares.

De corazón trato

ser monógamo

pero me aterra

la vida monocroma.

Obviamente monoteista,

mi Dios único,

soy incapaz de compartirlo.

Disculpa el monólogo,

trato de ser inclusivo.

Probar el diálogo

con una manada

de monos más monos

que yo,

aquellos que usan monóculos.

El tema será dualismo

eventualmente pluralismo.

Mi monograma~LD

Greed

Abraham Jaramillo

I hate
telling people
what to do,
as if they had no clue,
so I'm not here
to tell you how to chew,
here I am
just to tell you what I see,
and so
you are more than free
to leave,
for this is not a plea,
again,
I hate
telling people
what to do,
so here is my view.

It all started with the color blue,
yes,
a woman at a Wal-Mart
fighting

with another woman

for the last

blue dress,

yes,

bless

the poor,

underpaid store employee

who stops these types of fights,

then, someone writes

a generous check

to a government official;

having it

on video

is not enough these days,

let's be real,

faced with the choice

of less or more,

people will always choose

More.

One more bookstore closed

for a higher paying store front.

More,

motor cars turn into houses,

all in the name of higher paying tenants.

More,

crops that need more water in the desert

take over less profitable, yet more suitable, plants,

money in the banks is a must.

More,

a big CEO fires thousands of employees

to keep investors happy,

happiness is not always for all,

but what if

instead of More we choose

Less.

José Mujica,

Uruguay's president, gave away

90% of his monthly salary.

Mr. Mujica

drove an old, Volkswagen Beetle

and chose to live in a farmhouse

instead of

a presidential residence;

the richest president in my opinion.

Less,

God bless

Fray Tormenta,

a Mexican priest who became

a Lucha Libre Wrestler

to support an orphanage

for 23 years.

Less,

a daughter chooses

a blue dress

instead of an expensive wedding dress,

her mother's dress,

Less.

Hear Me

Felicia Taylor E.

You Monstrouls of the inner world

I am woman

And will be treated as I will

Will let. Will allow. Will stop

Or cut off your livelihood

Too long a time of the #MeToo

And the do what you want to do

Are you putrid, filled with power or wanton lust?

Then let us go at it together

Or kiss my stop, cease and deliver, as a harsh thrust

I am woman, hear me

I am man, feel me

I am human, let me breathe

My mother said a closed mouth won't get fed

And some things have been allowed, far too long

Standing upon my pedestal, I deliver this to you

Blowing my trumpet, like Louis Armstrong do
No acceptance of second class or second best

I've learned it's us that determine our own test
Pre-quizzes will no longer be embraced
A manifestation I've given for myself

Monstrouls of this inner world
Shake it left or right, I don't care

We've awakened to the dealing hand

Aayo

Gustavo R. Ramirez

In Southern California, just before *Cinco de Mayo,*
I celebrate a feast, invited by my loving Aayo.
My Aayo is my Aunt. She knows that she's my Tía.
We teach each other cultures, She learns about Pancho Villa.
We've had pyramids in Mexico. We have *La Catedral.*
They've been architectural masters. Even built the Taj Mahal.
We say, "Peace be with you." *Assalamualaikum.*
We teach each other languages. *Inlakech Alakin.*
You are another me. I am another you.
Fatima. Faduma. Our familial love is true.
You ask, "What is in a name?" like Mohammud ben Al-Ahmar
Abraham, Ishmael, Isaac. Even my *primo* Omar.
My mother Guadalupe. Mexico. America.
Your mother. The Muslim world. Somalia. North Africa.
Even Persian gardens. How many centuries it's been.
Algebra and alchemists. *Alfombras* of Aladin
Long before our times, Egyptians carved Alabaster
The influence is thine, from the novice to the masters.
There are mosques acting as churches. *Mezquita Cristo de la Luz*
Sometimes history is peaceful. But there are also violent truths.
From Arabia to Mexico, with the mystery of the crow.
Alameda. Cottonwood. "Remember the Alamo"

From Seville to Cordoba, from Mecca to Medina

The cities join together, as I connect to Aayo-Nina.

Aayo pays respect to Jesus. Special meaning of his birth.

Together we unite to work for Peace on Earth.

We must become best of friends. In the mosque or by the steeple.

Words of great Chief Joseph. "Send Rain... that all may be one people."

We're brothers and we're sisters. We're *familia*–family.

We've forever bonded. We weave a tapestry.

Lotería

Sanjuanita Martinez

"Este mundo es una bola y nosotros un balón!" se escuchaba cada fin de semana.

Gritábamos: ¡Buenas! O como aquí en este 'lado' se dice, "Loteria," "Bingo,"

Todo dependía de quién ganaba–joven o no tan joven.

Y así las costumbres pasaban de generación a generación.

La mesa estaba tupida de gente, mi gente.

Se escuchaba el sonido de fichas, frijol crudo, o monedas de valor

ó los pesos que poco a poco lo van perdiendo.

Y era todo un festín ya que hasta papá reclamaba sus cartas–las de la sirena, decía...

Mamá era la más tramposa–fingía ganar mientras papá iba dos o tres cartas atrás.

Y no era la meta quién ganaba más, pues si de eso se trataba seguro había inflación

pues un "nicle" o "nickel" era mucho que hasta regateábamos el precio de la carta.

Y así sucesivamente pasamos, sin pensarlo, la cultura, o la falta de ella, a los peques

ya que al final todos corrían para levantar las monedas caídas debajo de la mesa.

El ganador, se decía, que nadie lo quería por ese dicho que dice–afortunado en el amor, desafortunado en el dinero. Muchos como yo ni uno ni el otro.

Y seguimos con la esperanza de encontrar fortuna lejos de la mesa de mamá.

Fortuna en el amor es lo que se busca,

ya que en el dinero parece que jamás se encontrará.

Aunque aún así volvemos cada semana a probar la suerte

ó tal vez a confirmar que la fortuna en el amor un día llegará.

Al final eso es lo que somos–un balón.

Con todo y nuestras costumbres, tradiciones, e ideales

vamos por la vida rodando y rodando. Esperando.

Buscando dónde parar muy a pesar de las pateadas.

Siempre esperando el beso del famoso jugador.

Ó tal vez sigamos en el juego de lotería

Esperando el turno a gritar, "¡Buenas!"

Go Forward Please

Lois Jackson King

Don't dare to look back; look up! Looking back will throw you off track

The world is under stress; lot of hatred and lying facts

Too much of past thoughts, can cause heartaches and much pain

The knowledge of it all is what the enemy calls "Great" to fit their claim

Forward in unity and peace is to be our focus and our aim

Feeding not into the spirit and emotions of the evil's hand

YOUR present and your future, is at hand; encouraging each other to a firm stand

Use that which you have learned, even though it wasn't in the plan

All the hurt, loss of a loved one, and low in spirit, is not the end; reach out and become a friend

Be strengthened by the experience we have received

God will see us through if we have courage to proceed

Trust and believe; I am here, please take my hand

WE ARE IN THIS TOGETHER AND WILL BE UNTIL THE VERY END AND THEN SOME

Maybe U Can

dedicated to DSTL Arts family

Mauricio "Soul on Fire" Moreno

i can't make blueprints
for city shelters, can-
not raise roofs over
sunken eyes, nor can

i fill downtrodden souls
with hope, that
the city has not
abandoned them.

Maybe
You
Can

i can't sculpt gardens
out of milk thistles, can-
not penetrate Terra
with my fingers, nor can

i coax her to trust
me with her roses, that
they won't be crushed

under concrete blocks

Maybe

You

Can

i can't speak

Nahuatl or Chibcha, can-

not invoke the language

of my ancestors, nor can

i command my tongue

to resurrect the mysteries

of my skin, that it may

pass down its legends to my kin

Maybe

You

Can

i can't paint murals

on alleyway walls, can-

not fill spaces with

the colors of hope, nor can

i summon these shades
of white, green and red
to inspire generations, that they
may remember the faces of heroes

Maybe
You
Can

i can't photograph
the natural world, can-
not see the beauty of
deserts and tundras, nor can

i expose the world to the
majesty of life within
the frames of my Nikon, that we
may know our place on the planet

Maybe
You
Can

i can't speak love
in Japanese, can-

not see through Engineer
spectacles, nor can

i fall in love with poetry
as a child learning
how to fly, that she
may inspire us to live

Maybe
You
Can

i can't burn down
the patriarchy, can-
not bring about the
flames of change, nor can

i expose minds to
the absurdity of corrupt
systems and tyranny, that they
may fuel the sparks of tomorrow

Maybe
You
Can

i can't prepare
delicious meals, can-
not invoke my ancestors
with my food, nor can

i continue traditions
and honor the customs
of our culture, that they
may share wisdom with tomorrow

Maybe
You
Can

i can't comfort the sick
and dying, can-
not wrap I.C.U. patients
with warm blankets, nor can

i muster the strength
to look death in the
eye with a smile, that it
may bring solace in their final hour

Maybe

You

Can

i can't instill wisdom

to my daughter, can-

not watch her grow and teach her

how to live, nor can

i guide her with my actions

to be the change we

so desperately need, that she

may find the change in herself

Maybe

You

Can

i can't create fables

with words, can-

not conjure metaphors about

the need for connection, nor can

i weave tales of love

and longing to read, that they

may prove we are not alone

Maybe

You

Can

i can't paint with

watercolors, can-

not blend my visions and

dreams onto canvas, nor can

i heal myself through

art and inspire my children

to do the same, that they

may find strength to honor themselves

Maybe

You

Can

i can't raise a child

with special needs, can-

not love him or teach him

to make do, nor can

i give him the space

to smile at the world

without fear or shame, that they

may know he's a gift from God

Maybe

You

Can

i cannot change the world

Maybe

We

Can

stardust

Karyn Grasse

animal king, ghost

in a machine.

object of divine affection, architect

of your own destruction.

a universe between your atoms

– m o s t l y   e m p t y –

eternity wrapped in pulsating

muscle, encapsulated breath.

conscious of your own thoughts, aware

of your own demise.

the distant hope of your

ancestors, the progenitor of stories.

a random harmony of strings, held

together by improbability.

beholder of beauty and whisperer

of mysteries.

the universe is hardly aware of you, yet balances
on your very existence.

you shine like the stars, you are made
of them.

Who Am I?

Sanjuanita Martinez

A breath
With a pair of lungs
filled with hopes
Of keeping me afloat.
So they can take me
where I want to go.
And I go to places
Time after time
praying and hoping
For unstoppable function.

A breath
With cells glued together–
Sometimes not–
Take me through
Changes, phases
That I'd rather not–
Incessant changes
May bring on fear.
For change is not always good
"However inevitable,"
Like the saying goes.

A breath
With a hard-wired mechanism
Which monitors mobility,
Summons thought,
And plays me like a marionette,
Pulling on every string
While I fight a move or two.

A breath
With tiny active vessels
Which carry a rich crimson substance
Here and there
To replenish and renew
The successful
continuation
Of the show.

A breath
With one intricate device
Working night and day
Taking in and putting out
That dark substance
Flowing incessantly
Like the night traffic

on a busy street.

That which defines

One's outcomes

Happy or sad.

Yes, a breath

I long to have

But will one day

Cease to be.

I See You

Ani Minasian

there you are

I see you

behind your glowing

smile and saltwater tears

isolated from your nucleus of

friends and enemies

cut off from the messy drama of your life

deeper than your ideals and politics

underneath your traumas and fears

unburdened by memories, good or bad

light years away from your pipe-dreams and fantasies

there

speechless and radiant

a microscopic spark in a universe of suns and stars

flickering in your own infinitesimal orbit

distinct yet common

trivial yet precious

almost nothing

in the big scheme of things

yet somehow

everything

to me

Layers of a Generation

Felicia Taylor E.

Struggling to survive day by day
A structure built from their
hands and laboring

She calls it the home and shack, of
where she'll always be

No matter what they had, they'd give to
others, when they didn't have

Teaching me to keep
building and building up

The visions always been "to do better
when you know better."

And each generation gaining
more than the next

As hatred tried to stop the continuation,
when my Great-great Grandfather was
killed, left behind was his wife and child

It didn't stop the growth of our family
forged onward, with
truth and a solid will we survived

Each layer is built by generation
And brick by brick, we don't give
in and will never quit

Write and Wrong

Tina Fallon

I write because I want to share

I share so I can write

I read so I can write better

I write better because I read

I want to write about the reading process

I want to read about how to write

Reading helps me learn right from wrong

It's wrong not to read and write

I don't know what I enjoy more, reading or writing

I used to hate to write and I also hated reading

It's so hard to learn how to write and read

When you're learning English you begin to know what is right and wrong

In theater there is no right or wrong

In medicine you could make right and wrong choices

Right and wrong could be the difference between life and death

It's good to learn how to read and write the right way

It's wrong not to care

My Hands

Kathy Vega

I build and I create look at my hands, they have molded this earth.

I formed the beauty of the buildings that you use, they allow you
to work.

My working hands allow you to do what you need to do.

I thank you. I thank you for your working hands.

I see you. I see the dignity in your eyes.

Your working hands give me the space to do what I need to do.

I type and I type look at my hands, I have created spreadsheets
that provide data

I analyze with my brain and create data that allows you to see.

My working hands and my brain allow you to do what you need
to do.

I thank you. I thank you for your brain and for you data.

I am grateful to use my brain to strategize. I can see the diligence in your data.

Your data gives me the figures to do what I need to do.

We create with our hands, with our brains, with our hearts at times.

Are we all creating and receiving equally?

Poetic Exploration

Ani Minasian

Exploring the far
reaches of our
universe, mapping the uncharted
frontier where few, if any,
have gone before, unlocking
the secrets of our origins,
providing insights
into our future, probing
hidden corners and allowing
for the discovery
of sites or formations
otherwise difficult or impossible
to identify, targeting Venus
and Mars, reaching for stars,
seen and unseen… Poetry

is a mission
for the truly fearless
because this type of exploration
has come at a considerable cost,
with most failing before
completing their missions, some failing

before they even begin. This high failure

rate can be attributed
to the complexity and large
number of variables involved.
Still, proponents argue that
it can lead us to the extraction
of valuable resources
and some scientists say
it is necessary
for mankind to avoid
extinction. Perhaps

someday it will be
commonplace for all
individuals to use it for
the purpose of personal
discovery and recreation.

Person

Abraham Jaramillo

Cosmic dust turned into life,
one cell turned into five,
from the ocean to the land
natural selection created the gland
and the hand
with five digits,
but one–all of the sudden,
made it
special,
from grabbing a spear
to holding a beer,
cheers to the brilliance
of William Shakespeare
and E.L. James,
diversity of taste runs through its veins
and sometimes other chemicals,
such a busy mind seeks ways to escape,
video games sometimes
let it be someone other than,
after all a nine-to-five
can drive anyone crazy,
in a normal house of five

in a city of millions

in this world of billions

you are...

Seven Stars in Heaven

Gustavo R. Ramirez

Part 1: The Genesis

When stars ask you questions

Answer them!

"Where do you stand with your God?"

They say, "We carry the wisdom."

"We are the word."

"We are the consciousness who suggested,

'Let there be light.'"

(And there was light.)

(And God saw that the light was good.)

"What are you up to?"

"What are you here for?"

"Do you know your mission?"

"What is your purpose in life?"

When we live out our mission with our hearts full of love, alongside, co-creating and manifesting God's will, we edify ourselves and the stars. When we edify our mission, we consecrate it. We connect with the stars and with God. We edify the stars.

I am the son of Sun.

The son of man.

The sun of sons.

The sun of suns.

The son of Stars.

The sun of Stars.

Atum of all the stars.

Creator of avatars

... Because he was lonely...

We were lonely too.

Avatars among the stars

Avatar of avatars

Children so profoundly right as they wonder what you are

Stellae try to reach us from afar.

Part 2: Star Sisters

When I was small and innocent I trusted you,

I even bought a telescope to find Haley's Comet among the Pleiades.

But I never found you.

Don't be too concerned: I had already become used to your empty promises.

They call you the Pleiades.

My Dad calls you *Las Siete Hermanas*–the Seven Sisters

I call you my Star Sisters

Because we come from the same mother.

Because I, like you, am made of stardust.

Because we are all stardust.

(But stardust blows away)

Part 3: Live Heaven on Earth

Star light

Star bright

First Star I see tonight.

Everything else was a darker shade of grey.

LET THERE BE BLACK

She molded the seven continents.

Then God created man.

We edify African mother

I edify black sister

Castaway in America.

(Their faces glimmer in heaven.)

So we say their names.

"We are all Africans."

–D. Huerta

Meanwhile, I bought a star for Dolores.

She's going strong

We are going strong

Our mission is to uplift.

Our purpose is to edify each other.

So we hold up our Star Sisters.

The Star Parents

Star Children

The I'itoi Messiahs

And the Brothers of the Sun

Stellae

Sisters of the Morning Star

La Estrella de la Mañana

El Lucero del Amanecer

Madre de Dios

Las tres Marias

Seven Stars in Heaven

Mujer

Autoridad

The healing people

As we lift each other up,

we edify all stars.

We manifest our Mission.

Peace and Love abound.

And,

At long last,

the *distanced* universe *Hugs,*

and We Live Heaven On Earth

The Promise

Sanjuanita Martinez

Beloved

It is for you; It is for me.

It is for all to see.

Don't be fearful

For the Promise exists.

Don't despair.

It will not be long before we can all rejoice

In this Covenant made.

Yes, it is a cold world–angry, sad, selfish–

With deep scars,

But this too shall pass.

In the meantime,

Make the "now" matter.

Do not wait... love!

Love as deep as the oceans.

Walk along the shore and speak

For He listens.

Take deep prolonged breaths.

Feel the breeze as it whispers your name.

Gaze at the twinkling stars

As they spell your name across the sky.

Yes, Beloved,

Await the promise.

And love.

Word Food

for Ani

David Fallon

Her talk of feeding us
with her words
a meal of understanding
and feeling
and betterment
of the soul inspires
my own recipe

I want my words
to be like the humble
sandwich

The complex meat more
than savory and sweet dances
on the tongue and in
the brain creating meaning beyond
mere words

Lettuce like the earth
a delight that poses
questions about our being
and who we are

in the universe

Tang of tomato
the operatic star of the show
taking the spotlight before
succumbing to harmony

Onion's sting
a peppery aroma
that heightens all others
like the spare
but well-placed adverb

The necessary but forgotten
condiments
lining the vessel
like sentences on pages
form and function combined

And of course the bread
rich and hearty
in some cultures a meal
in itself the sum of human
ingenuity individual ingredients
combined to manifest

a strong whole

The meal of words

not to be ignored

first feeds the face

then feeds the soul

Unity Wheel

Kathy Vega

Within the depths of my soul I have known.

I have heard the words: "All men are created equal."

I feel the unity in the word men. I would even venture "all humans are created equal."

Todo ser humano es igual.

So there is no confusion,

No worries for exclusion;

The message has been clear. It was clear as children, it was clear as a bright sky with no clouds.

Join me in this celebration of La Rueda, the wheel.

Explore with me, join me in this journey. Síganme, no se queden atrás.

We look to the four directions for guidance: EAST, WEST, SOUTH, NORTH.

We enter in the East: Fire, Fuego, Nina, Honesty.

We allow the Fire of honesty to purify everything. El Fuego de honestidad purifica todo. Honesty allows us to see the truth. Be brave and listen to the pain of one another. Be brave and hear the voices and cries of all our fears, abandonments, betrayals, wounds, loss, grieving, all the hurt, listen... And allow it to burn.

We move to the West: Mother Earth, Madre Tierra, Pachamama. STRENGTH.

La fuerza de Madre Tierra que con su sabiduría nos abraza. Who holds us in her arms. Pachamama who has heard our cries and holds us with strength. The mother who knows to nurture us as we rebuild and recreate, renew. She knows all. She knows we can move toward this new creation of new knowledge. She knows our beauty. Ella sabe lo bello que somos y con su fuerza nos ama. She loves us with all her strength. We are not alone.

With our renewed strength,

We come to the South: Water, Ague, Unu. COMPASSION.

We swim in the ocean of compassion. En el mar de compasión nadamos. Feel the truth of compassion. The pure, unconditional love that we find for ourselves and for each other. I look in your eyes brother, sister, mother, daughter, son, and know you are me, and I am you. Veo en tus ojos la verdad. La verdad del amor sin condiciones. Love without conditions. Unconditional love. We now know.

Our hearts are full and we are just about ready to fully unite with you. Time to go North. ¡Vamos para el Norte!

Norte: Air, Aire, Wayra.

We find the air of understanding in the North; in the mind. The knowledge of what has brought us here. The understanding of who we are, how we can create. The air we breathe in, and out, gives us information and power to communicate, to learn more. We bring it all together in deep wisdom. This wisdom informs us how we will walk together, como caminaremos juntos. There is safety in this air of understanding. Bringing us to full joy.

We thank the directions East, West, South, North, Este, Oeste, Sur, Norte.

We thank the elements Fire, Earth, Water, Air, Nina, Pachamama, Unu, Wayra.

We thank them all for bringing us together and reintegrating our new truth, which is our old truth. That all humans are created equal. We have arrived at Unity. Unidad, Ipa.

Prophecy Resurrected—Our Rallying Cry

Gustavo R. Ramirez

Inspired by Malcolm X, Martin Luther King, Jr., Roy Duarte, Bill Wilson, "Doctor Bob," Lupe Reyes Ramirez, Maria Elena Chavez, Dolores Huerta, Kathryn Kirui, David Fallon, Jerry Hoffman, Anonymous Hopi Elder, Gustavo Gutierrez, Rafael Reyes, Octavio Ramirez, Jose Z. Calderon, Jeanette Royston, & Luis A. Pichardo

We are not just fighting for our personal rights. We are advocating, praying, educating, singing, travelling, uniting, rallying, fasting, inspiring.

WE ARE YELLING AS ONLY THE DYING CAN SCREAM.

With FIERCE URGENCY, We are willing to put our differences aside & to unite on common ground, as HUMANITY. This very moment is that fateful time in which we must accept and act on the fact that we are headed toward annihilation. As you, I and the worldwide community weave movements together, we emerge stronger. We are the saviors we've been waiting for. We must and will transform our planet—in fact we are transforming Planet Earth by our committed, divine thought and action now. We are Marching... No Longer by Ones and Twos, but in Legions of Millions. We March Onward & UPWARD,

making Manifest the Very Right, Indeed, the PROPHECY
Of OUR SACRED MOTHEREARTH

to EXIST.

Providence wills us to survive... and to THRIVE

Latest News!

Sanjuanita Martinez

Women have been more likely than men
to show adverse reactions to writing poetry.

Seventy-nine percent of these women
Have reported that they still want to write
Regardless of outcome.
They claim that writing poetry
Has saved their lives
Despite adverse reactions.

They also claim that
everyone can benefit
Since, without poetry,
life can be difficult
And unbearable.

Writing poetry has helped them feel safe
and accepted by those who have done the same.
Therefore, no matter the cost or the tears,
Writing poetry is a lifesaver.

Men see the benefit, too.

Therefore, they must also continue writing

because if we unite in this endeavor,

we will make this a healthier

and happier life.

Part III

Michelle Smith

Eating my envy

With pizza and coke

Domino's on speed dial is not a joke

And is envy too strong of a word that reveals

My hobbies and classes have ceased

Since I have become a cog in the working wheel

Hectic hours of the AM shift float to the PM

since CM's have called off

How much more can I take of this shit,

I mean shift,

No I truly mean shit

As in an ADL assistance and the change of an incontinence brief

Even the seniors call them diapers

Not Depends or Always

Damn it's 4:30 am and time escapes me

Stolen from the sandman thief

Drinking my envy from a glass of

chilled Cupcake Chardonnay

The 13 percentage dazes me and

I hear have another drink in my head

In eight hours I shall gallop like a horse

To the racetrack

With blinders to the starting gate

As I the jockey prepare for the

Win, place, or show

Trot my hooves on the smooth gravel and dirt

Run like my life depends on it

For the win, place, or show

Sliding

Tina Fallon

Sliding into reality
though reality is here
Would anybody notice
if I quit
acknowledging the day?

Creating one's own future
achieving the goals you want
What if you don't belong
in this reality? What if
you don't feel reality?
What if
life is a scam?
What if
I'm already dead and I'm in
some sort of limbo? I wonder
how I died? An accident? Was I
murdered and still have that
unfinished business? No,
if I was in limbo, I would probably
already know how
I died. No, wrong

again. Limbo is a place

of the undecided destiny. Back

to the drawing board, back

to reality.

¡Marcha!

Gustavo R. Ramirez

We were at war. Desert Storm. Iraq.

Before this war, my mother watched and cried as my older brother left from high school to the military. The few. The proud.

I was sad, but I wasn't scared.

Over 15 years later, in December of 2005, Univision reported on HR 4437, the Sensenbrenner Immigration Bill. So draconian that it would make felons out of reverends who knowingly shared the sacred host with "illegal aliens". It would make felons out of ambulance drivers who knowingly transported those "illegals."

My heart dropped with fear.

"These are my students!"

"I must do something! But what can I do? I'm not a governor or congressman. I'm not even a mayor. I'm just a teacher." That night, after hours of tossing and turning, I had the worst nightmare.

The next morning I thought it had all just been a dream, until Telemundo and other stations reported the bill had passed in the Senate, and could very well pass the House. For the first time in my life, an event on the news made me tremble with fear. And in just 19 minutes I had to be strong for my students–adult, English as a Second Language students, who were my heroes.

They had stepped up to help restore lives and give hope to the survivors of Hurricane Katrina, just months before–in unprecedented, brilliantly creative ways. They were recognized for their valor by the Red Cross, Salvation Army, and Central American Hurricane Relief. They had self-advocated for citizenship and emergency training classes. Earlier in the week, Maricruz, a new arrival from Michoacán, had just ended her short class speech with, "We now have hope." I was thinking about this all as I parked, trying to collect myself to retain their hope.

The words of the late Harvey Milk resonated in my memory as I sweat. "I know you cannot live on hope alone. But without it life is not worth living. And you. And you (I felt as if he was talking straight at me from his holy gravesite). You gotta give'm hope." I looked at my watch. I had two minutes before meeting my students for class.

"Breath, Gus. Everything's gonna be alright."

Maybe we can start another coalition.

But Hurricane Katrina was different, and they were seen as heroic in that endeavor.

Now they're practically being called vermin.

Ok, Gus. Breathe. Look confident, and fake it till you make it.

With a (pretend) smile.

Ready… Set… And… Action!

"Teacher! Teacher!!

I can do it.

You can do it.

He can do it.

She can do it.

They can do it.

We can do it!"

The voice of God.

The voice of God, coming in the form of student Patricia.

Patricia was finally and proudly able to repeat aloud last week's lesson. And loud she was.

Si, se puede. Yes, we can.

Dolores Huerta had "coined" Si, se puede years ago in Arizona, my mother had told me.

Dolores exclaimed an emphatic, "Si se puede," when all the men around her said that it couldn't be done. My mother had taught me about Dolores Huerta and my Tías and Tíos confirmed her successful tactics.

I thought in a split second, if Dolores could be so effective as a young Chicana decades before me (and was still going strong), then my tried and tested Pomona heroes could and would step up to the plate now.

And together, we did.

We began a seedling organization almost overnight. We were strategic in the name: the Coalition for Safety and Well-being. This would even go far beyond the civics requirement of the class.

Within days we were off to Pomona City Hall, prepared speeches in hand, while knowing we were speaking from the heart.

The mayor gave us the cold shoulder at City Hall, as she and the council resolved a certainly much more pressing dog dispute. Vice Mayor Marco Robles was the only council member to help us that first day.

The plan was to join the cities of Maywood and Huntington Park, California, and help build a local-to-national movement to stop HR 4437, and then to provide a well-earned route to citizenship. I quickly got in contact with the mayor of Huntington Park and council members of Maywood. But we were in for an uphill battle. Among other factors, the demographics of those cities were very different from those of Pomona. For example in Maywood and Huntington Park the ethnic make up was almost 100% Latino, as opposed to the more diverse Pomona.

This is when I reached out for more local help. Activist and friend, Jerry Hoffman was always first on my list and he began helping immediately by researching how Pomona could maximize our legal system. The city attorney began asking Jerry for answers, and Jerry was quick to provide them (often in the middle of city hall meetings, to the Pomona attorney's embarrassment). Organizer extraordinaire, Arturo Jimenez, introduced me to the Pomona San Gabriel Valley Latino and Latina Roundtable. I knew that if they got on board, well...

"This is history. Write this down. Gustavo, document this."

These are the words spoken to me from prominent activist, author, and professor Jose Calderon in April of 2006. "Our students are going to shape history."

When I went to the Latin@ Roundtable, Profe Calderon said that we should begin right after the Cesar Chavez Pilgrimage of 2006. But I told the Roundtable that the House would vote before the pilgrimage, and that we had only a few weeks to stop this bill from passing. There was a vote, and the Roundtable became involved immediately, and powerfully.

Meanwhile, I was going to meetings of Coalición 27 de Marzo in Los Angeles to help plan a "megamarch" so large, it would send a huge message of the power of Latinos, immigrants and allies. I went to Los Angeles city council meetings, where I began to speak with Councilman Eric Garcetti (now, the Mayor of L.A.) We felt that if Pomona would become a so-called "sanctuary city" through a resolution, and if L.A. followed, then this would begin an avalanche of other cities and government entities putting pressure on the House to "kill the bill."

"De colores se visten las flores en la primavera…" We all held hands and sang. After much work and people power, a resolution in support of the undocumented and against HR 4437 passed in Pomona Hall at the council meeting. Hundreds of people cheered loudly even in the rain, as there was a huge overflow of attendees. Media showed up en masse and ran with the story. The very next day, Los Angeles passed a similar resolution.

From Coachella Valley to the ocean, we were also focussed on creating the "megamarcha." We must thank Chicago for blowing up the standard and organizing a march of 300,000 people. The multi-organization Coalición 27 de Marzo chose Saturday for the march, but the United Farmworkers Union (UFW) was non-negotiable about having it on Sunday, being that Saturday was a workday for so many. The radio and television stations announced the Saturday march at every chance. Some leaders of the Coalición 27 began to be emboldened to predict one million people. I had already learned that up to that date the largest marches in L.A. history were of about 100,000 people (against the Vietnam War and against infamous Proposition 187). Having had a humble hand in Los Angeles' march against 187 and many other marches of far less attendees, I must admit I had doubts that we would make a million people, for that would be 10 times bigger than the largest marches of L.A., ever.

"Shoot for the stars, and you'll land in the heavens," was my motto, and I wanted to unify both marches by staying overnight and welcoming the UFW rally the next day. Even if "only" hundreds were to do this, it would send the strongest of messages of commitment and solidarity to the world.

I had never seen anything like I did on March 27, 2006. It was nothing like the record march against 187. Every street and every sidewalk, in all directions from Los Angeles City Hall were crowded, shoulder-to-shoulder, with people as far as the eye could see. One famous international reporter was even weeping with tears of shock and joy, off the set, because she didn't think such an action was even in the realm of possibility.

Even police officers, who were friendly with us, told me that with a crowd that big the only thing they could do was "ride it out," and let it happen peacefully. One officer told me, "We don't have the capacity to halt a rally this big." He said, "Just like in Pomona, most of us are with you all in spirit, anyway–just be non-violent, please. Please." I remember he emphatically said please twice regarding the non-violence. No one wanted rioting. It went down in history as a totally peaceful march, and by far the largest march in L.A. history. Authorities initially estimated 300,000 to 500,000 people, but according to aerial views and other research, the crowd was well over a million strong.

The bill was killed that day. Lessons were learned.

Lesson #1: You can beat city hall. On the first appearance at Pomona, the mayor and all of the council members, except one, were against our request. On the final vote, the mayor and council voted with us. This brings us to:

Lesson #2: You can bring city hall along with you and affect much greater change.

Lesson #3: A tiny handful of people can help inspire an entire metropolis into action in a short amount of time. It was hard to believe that the councils of Maywood, Huntington Park and Pomona, along with a few not-so-famous and unrecognized activists, could inspire Pasadena and Los Angeles to officially express solidarity and pave the way for a nation... Hard to believe, but true.

Here to Serve You

Kathy Vega

I am the hostess Love ME

I will serve you Love ME

Aquí estoy para servirTe

"Boy, take my apples, leaves, branches, logs until I am a stump"

This is what I know

Aprendí ser una buena mujer

Mujeres buenas sirven as su familia

YES! This is what I learned a good woman does,

She learned that being a good woman serves her family

Don't think I am bad, please, when I don't have a family to serve

I will serve you in place

No quiero ser la mala, I don't want to be bad

Just let me be here to serve you, let me be here to give to you

To give the best party, to give the best dinner, I want you to be in joy

Even though I was anxious, even though I will be in debt

Let me serve you so that you can Love Me!

Aquí estoy para servir, ÁmaMe!

I Feel like a Cog in the Machine/Am I Married to My Job?

Michelle Smith

I feel like a cog in the machine

A robot with moves

Of strength and sustainable steel

Put back

Output

Input

Build again

Oil my machine

Replenish me

Bend back and forth

My steel can only take so much more

Machinery breaks down

Factors break down

Multiples build up

Is my employment a math equation?

I am married to my job

I am its greatest defender

In all the glory and splendor

There's woe and wonder

Will I become like them?

Walker, wheelchair, or rollator bound

Assisted shower dependent

Or walk to the patio with independence

I move about at a brisk pace and on my feet 95 percent

I hear and see a 101 year old quoting Proverbs 3:5-6

And happily singing lyrics for Amazing Grace how sweet the sound

She is the church and my revival

Good God thank you for this survival

I am married to my job and don't want a divorce?

My heart, patience, and drive

Reflects in my work ethic

A deserved paycheck is not all I see

There are residents the same age as my mom and dad, they are dearly departed,

I have cried wishing I could comb her hair or select a suit and tie for dinner

And eventually I will take a 10 minute break sit down

I am married to my job

A bit more than I should be

Happily with integrity

Shoes Could Talk

Lois Jackson King

Oh man, didn't we have an exciting time last night

And I say, I was brightly shining in the night; and you too looked alright

That place was really jumping; food and music was out of sight

But what happened later, was enough to say let's get out of here

There was shouting; "open up", plus a lot of banging on the door

Did you see how those shoes were moving all over that floor?

Some even went under the gambling tables and behind doors

Oh man, wasn't it funny how people started running

Amazing how some through the open window they went

A few of them was so scared they couldn't even think which way to go

Fear set in and many got caught; and into the police van they were sent

I am so glad we hid behind the room's partition

While the police looked around completing their mission

Yes, old friend, we were able to make it home, from which we started

So to you, my fellow friend, we are alright;

Thanks for wearing me, and I am still shining bright

And I believed, I fit you just right

Bricks

Tina Fallon

Weighing me down
Like a ton

of bricks, "don't look
out the window" they won't get

here any faster
Watch a show or play

with a toy, "please don't climb
or jump over your friends"

"I don't allow throwing (of any kind) inside the classroom"
"keep your hands to yourself don't punch

or yell
Use inside voices"

While I'm stuck in this hell
You might say, I'm

over it

'Cause I wanna go

home, but the sooner

I'm off, the less

money I'll make

Change of schedule

My lame complaints

Am I an educator

or a glorified

babysitter?

A Simple Walk on The Twilight of the Pandemic

March 20th, 2021

Karyn Grasse

It's the middle of March, 2021, and I decided to go for a commemorative walk. The sun was low in the sky and shadows were growing very long. I select a mask and a scarf in the hopes of keeping my face and neck warm. As I start out the door, I notice that my neighbor's house has a large SUV parked outside. They must have guests. Probably their adult children. They are seniors, and now fully vaccinated. And able to see family again. I feel happy for them. The isolation of the pandemic had been hard on them. We used to talk to each other from across the street on our cell phones. *Did their children get the vaccine too?*

Suddenly I am aware of my own bicep. It's as if someone had spent the night punching it. I had gotten my second dose of Pfizer the day before. But other than the punched-up arm and feeling a little tired, I was fine. The walk would do me good. As I start down the sidewalk, I notice a woman coming towards me, masked up and head-phoned up, and walking briskly. There's no room to give her space. Cars are parked solidly on the side of the road, leaving only a strip of sidewalk to walk on. We pass each other quickly and awkwardly. She is in her own little sound bubble and I don't intrude.

I notice a family down the street. Their kids are playing happily with a large rubber ball in the middle of the quiet street while the adults are keeping watch for approaching cars. The familiar phrase "Car coming!" rings out. Moments later a car whizzes by. A lady with a phone strapped to her arm is walking on the other side of the street, headphones firmly planted in-ear. A mask is dangling from her fanny pack. On the other block, a family of three are going for a stroll. They have matching blue surgical masks, the kind you buy in a multi-pack from Costco. They don't seem to be in any particular hurry.

Just then, a woman in a neck gaiter came around the corner, walking towards me at quite a clip. I step into the street to give her room to pass. We nod silently at each other. Every half minute or so a car goes past, vrooming into the silence of the evening and then moving on. A family is loading up two kids into their sedan, trying to keep the littlest one from running into the street. They look a little harried. In the distance a lady is walking her dog. It is colder than I had anticipated and I shove my hands deeper into my pockets, wishing that I had brought gloves.

From somewhere I hear "Daddy! Daddy!" It takes me a moment to realize that the voice is not my kid. I'm too far away from home at this point. Somewhere a child and their father are playing, I can hear the squeals and the laughter–but I cannot locate them in space. I assume it is coming from one of the backyards, but thanks to the hills and the acoustics, it is impossible to tell where. The sound seems like it is hanging in front of me. The child and father feel like ghosts. I am shaken out of my reverie by a woman walking toward me. She is sporting what is apparently today's required combo of mask and headphone. *Another?* But then I realize that I am wearing a mask and headphones too. *Guilty.* I step into the street to give her room to pass. She does not make eye contact. I mumble hello.

A man on the opposite corner is smoking an oversized cigarette (or small cigar?) and walking two medium-sized, eager dogs. Plumes of blue-white smoke emanate from his mouth. There is no evidence of a mask in his possession. I notice that he is white. That's unusual in this neighborhood, so I take a side glance to double check. He notices and nods at me. I smile stiffly and hurry on. Down the street someone else is walking their dog. She has a black bandana in her hair and a full black mask on her face. Only her eyes are showing. To me, she looks like she could be a super-hero. I imagine her bravely protecting the world from people who won't wear masks. This makes me smile. Overhead a jet is quietly making contrails in the empty, cloudless evening sky.

My Beloved Spirit

Kathy Vega

As a child I heard your voice. Escuche tu voz de niña.

Calling me. Llamándome.

I felt you deep in my heart. Te sentí profundamente en mi corazón.

Estoy segura con tu presencia. I am safe with your presence.

Guide me. Guíame.

Feed me. Dame de comer.

I follow you with my entire being. Te sigo con todo mi ser.

Dearest beloved spirit I am yours. Querido espíritu amado soy
tuya/o

With you I am whole. Contigo estoy entera.

She Has a Cat

for Karo

David Fallon

She has a cat that looks like ours
only it's not ours
but it looks so much like ours
that I can't help imagining it is

I make up stories about what
our cat is doing with her, what
he is getting away with when we are
not around to see

He probably likes it better there
because her hands are graceful
she has a soft voice
and she smiles more than we do

Maybe she feeds him better snacks
gives him lots of catnip
and he gets to lay on her bed
which he never gets to do here

And he probably gets to go outside
whenever he wants

to chase mice and catch birds
and happily in the dirt

I'm sure he really enjoys being
at her house and away from us
but probably not for long

because it's not his home

The Fruits of Life

Lois Jackson King

Words challenging–sounds different somehow; positive dreams yet sometimes nightmares; can't let it stop you now. Hi neighbor, can I be of service? Old, past bricklayer continues to help; so let's spread the production and enhance the worth and value toward tomorrow.

Developing and manufacturing dreams and imaginational designs. Here and there, all of us from everywhere; laying one brick at a time; greatness, we have, and will continue to achieve. We have each other's back; for the old and the young and all in-between.

Struggles, reevaluation, sometimes needed; some fall down; we help them up again, and again. We will continue to stand and to form, enrich and create far beyond–to make whole; from start to finish making level ground.

No big "I" or little "You;" we together in a forward move, each step a developing thought, ideas, creating, inventing, improvements, collaboration, unity in spirit, technology, scientific growth, reproduction from then to present.

Including and incorporating, Faith, Hope, open and secret prayer; taking each moving step to the "mat;" building solid brick-like foundations, by each and every individual's involvement and contribution. The path for bricklaying shall never cease–always a new way, a better way to learn.

Cassettes to CD's; VHS to DVD's, rabbit-ears to cable, then to digital; just as the world continues to turn; our bricklayer's development shall increase and grow; and you can get involved.

Think about it; no test to take, unlimited talent and gifts of creation, no riddles to solve.

Welcome, welcome, welcome; come, there is so more to be done and we need you.

You can make the choice, let us together help too; and lay a brick or even two.

Part IV

Michelle Smith

A cog in the working wheel

And I am a tired zombie of repetition

Same thing different day, evening, or night

Will I have it any other way?

Am I expendable?

Certainly I am beyond dependable

And my CNA license proves that I am capable

Envy from the devourer of cherry cheesecake pairs with a glass of ice cold milk

I laugh about Rhinestone and ILK

aka Trump's brown-nosers Diamond and Silk

And what are they doing these days?

They can't hold a candle to me,

Their wick would burn out anyway

Unify

Gustavo R. Ramirez

I thought I was a unifier, but what I did was protest
Fancied myself a servant-leader. Put each other to the test.

I'd never cower, I wouldn't hide.
but what I did was just divide.

I feared the cops detested me. I was too much to handle.
And now I stand on sacred ground as I take off my sandals.

Forty days and forty nights–I listened, learned and prayed.
Today I am a newer man. I stand upright today.

We learn to give and learn to live, although we still will stumble.
I'm no better than you–you, no better than me. I aim to be forever humble.

You say mosque. I say church. He burns sage. She hears bells of steeples.
We need unifiers–human angels. Heart to heart. And we will save our people.

I am Mexican indigenous. The first Americans.
But there's no you separate from I. There's we like, "Yes we can."

We means you and I… loved former enemies and mended fences

We healed our hurts and we forgave. Gave up our differences.

As in a common shipwreck, we are birds of a feather.

Our differences make us alike. We can only do this together.

He was a peasant; you called them vermin. King said, "Off with their heads."

But when both black and white men bleed, they bleed the color red.

I'd like to be your servant-leader. Maybe you can be mine.

And give respect to all nature. God, all the glory is thine.

You may call me a dreamer, but it's not "pie in the sky."

If there's just one thing to do: Muster all strength and Unify.

So I will lead and I will follow in our land of the brave.

And one by one–one at a time, this whole wide world we'll save.

Question

Lois Jackson King

Where can I be placed, many marks have I made

Globetrotting I have done; it was one of my trade

In my space; environment–a picture of betrayal

What is to fill this vessel, a mere portrait–vapor or what

Framed trash position; forceful opinions–a change of mind

My life may be half-full, but it's better than considering that it
may be only half empty

I will survive; through all my situations it is not to be my destination

I am not alone–other's back turned; yet I have not been forsaken

Brotherly unity is in the midst of it all; you help me roll my log

I'll help roll yours; the highway of life we'll journey together

One elevation here and one over there

On one accord making each step count to the betterment of all

The World Needs Love

Sanjuanita Martinez

The World is hurting more every day.
No matter where we turn.
People are feeling ignored, cast away.
And nobody seems to acknowledge it.
Nobody seems to care.

When out in the streets, we tend to go our way
In the face of injustice.
Somebody else's business, not yours, not mine.
We may become curious and may just watch,
Or simply walk away.

Right before our eyes,
there is hunger, suffering, despair.
Right before our us
Is a world falling apart,
Where "if you are not like me,
Then I don't like you."
Where our hearts have become cold
and selfish;
Where we feel the center of our universe

This world is pleading,

searching, and thirsting

for love.

The world is in need of love.

Right beside our comforts

We hear cries through walls.

We hear the elderly in their solitude.

We hear the sick in their agony.

We hear the abandoned in their despair.

We hear the abused in their pain.

We hear the unborn in their torment.

Nothing. Nothing is done.

We just keep on...

What has become of us?

Who do we live for?

What do we live for?

What must **WE** do?

What must **I** do?

What can heal our world?

The power lies within us.

We can love.

We must love.

But we must first Listen.

Quiet down for a moment.

Slow down and listen

To those around you…

You have the power.

Offer your company, your ear

To those who need you.

Listen to those calling your name.

Offer yourself to those in need.

Bring joy to the sad.

Feed the hungry.

Care for the sick.

Be the voice for

the voiceless.

Let us build a better world.

Let us build each other up.

The world is you.

The world is me.

Listen. Love.

Your Life Matters

Gustavo R. Ramirez

Black Lives Matter. All Lives Matter. This we know: *We say.*

But if black lives really matter to you, you would join with me today.

Just open your eyes. Open your heart. It shouldn't have to be a riddle.

My heart broke when I awoke to the boy who just wanted, of all things, Skittles.

I heard Obama preachin' Dolores Huerta's "Si Se Puede; Yes We Can."

Over the backdrop of four little girls killed in Birmingham.

Police dogs attacked. People fought back. They took *La Causa* further.

You call it law and order, but the People call it, "murder."

See,

Can't sleep 'cause my heart's droppin'.

I hear whispers of guns cockin'.

CIA's crack and coke's poppin'.

White lines blowin'

Roosters crowin'

You get promotions while your shit's showin'.

To protect and serve. Not always what it seems.

Days are hot and the nights are mean.

Wanna shoot and let off our steam.

Hate begets hate so a truce is seen.

Black Lives Matter. Your Life Matters. This We Know. We Pray.

If my brother's life really mattered to you, you would join with us today.

See, our lives matter, and your life matters,

So please take the noose out of your rope.

Our brothers' lives don't take away from yours. So please–I get desperate for hope.

Don't be afraid to say "black lives." We've seen too many halos.

I see four little girls shining above. Yet, sometimes there are rainbows.

And if the world forgets me, please remember just one thing:

It's that YOUR LIFE MATTERS. What matters is dignity.

So to build that Rainbow in the sky

We don't need a magic ladder.

All I takes is for you to look into my eyes and tell me

"Your life matters."

Love thy Neighbor: Step by Step

Luz Donis

First: Define neighbor ie.

all of you, you all, y'all.

Second: Try not to dislike y'all.

Third: Take no offense to y'all's differences.

Fourth: Make a humongous blanket and cover y'all.

Fifth: Those on the extreme right or left, and other outliers tend to be discounted or outcast. Tuck them back in with care.

Sixth: Watch y'all morph.

Seventh: Stitch letters L-O-V-E on the blanket.

Vibration of the Spirit

Lois Jackson King

Come forth–Words unfold, rise high and clear.

Rise and meet the overflowing of your inner being

Allow every given space to be occupied

Receive posturing visions of hope; encouragement reaching beyond and past brokenness

Intriguing the intellect of capability; keeping "Arriba y no abajo" "Above and not below"

Encouraging toward appreciation of self-worth

Let us all (centrarse en seguir adelante), focus on going forward

Willing to work together; improving on what we have

Less attention given to what we don't have

We will soar high as the God-given sky; yes, we will fly

Peace and harmony will lead the way

Corrupt thoughts produce corrupt hearts

We must not allow self to follow trails of corruptness

Never shall corrupt be our way to ever flow–

We will speak with a clear conscience

Blotting out the crooked which may cause one to stumble and fall

Our pain will not cripple the cognition of the mind

The aim is doing it through peace of mind

We won't initiate words causing confusion

Working together for a better today, tomorrow, and life to come for all

Mortified

Tina Fallon

I have noticed

that there has been

an occurrence of

ciationlang

People have been using it

to communicate, write

songs: rock, pop & rap......

And in our schools.

Some people will learn it.

Some will research it

to no end

And some

will succumb to it

subconsciously.

Here are a few examples;

"On accident"

instead of

"By accident"

"Supposibly"

instead of

"Supposedly"

"Li bary"

Instead of

"Library"

"I feel like..."

instead of

"I think..."

"My bad"

Instead of

"Oops!"

This is the age

of ciationlang.

You do it, you learn it, become it

or simply

get kicked

to the curb

mortified.

Inspiration Studies

Kathy Vega

Our body needs Inspiration to be alive, that is a fact.

If you aren't inspired, you can inspire.

If you don't inspire, you die. Si no inspiras, te mueres.

Studies found that shallow inspiration leads to lack of sleep, fatigue, body pain and worse:

*DISENGAGEMENT from life. *ROMPIMIENTO de la vida.

Causes of shallow inspiration are anxiety, stress, illness and inability to create.

What can we do to prevent this?

We must work on mindful inspiration.

Practicing deep, inspiring techniques can help you with your disengagement.

Techniques include:

Find a place that is comfortable to do your inspiration exercises

The mountains, the oceans, the forest, a beautiful museum, your favorite room in your home.

Encuentra tu espacio.

Practice deep inspirations: instead of watching court tv, try observing nature, people, go on a picnic, travel, etc.

Tiempo de inspirar profundamente.

Next, inspire through your nose, let your belly fill all the inspirations.

Hold them inside while they grow and expand.

Then, release your inspiration and inspire the world.

Inspire others to create art, build movements, educate, design new buildings, innovate, and most of all, LOVE.

Cuando inspiras das AMOR!

**Disengagement–Removal from the present and self*

**Rompimiento–Quebrando del presente y de uno mismo*

A Touch of Heaven

Gustavo R. Ramirez

As I grow in recovery more will be revealed.

Sometimes I feel the pain. Sometimes I feel healed.

I knew not of humility–just ego, pride and vanity.

Now I know of hope. I have a chance at sanity.

I used to attract chaos and end up in disgrace.

Now I attract solutions, and I end up in grace.

I prayed broken hallelujahs. I felt betrayed and asked God, "Why?"

Today I pray the addict's prayer. I spread my wings and fly.

Not all moments are bliss, but they say, "Solo por hoy."

It's one day at a time, as I have a sense of joy.

I used to see the differences. Now I see my brethren.

As I listen to the message, I feel a touch of heaven.

shot

Karyn Grasse

a vial of No

More Fear slowly empties

into my arm & i

can stop running

away from my fellow

humans & maybe one

day we can even

Embrace.

Hope

Lois Jackson King

Am I here and am I there; (estoy aquí) therefore I am everywhere

I can feel, but can I be felt, many heart-breaking times

Beautiful sun-shiny days; with much darkness of heart

What is the greatness of tearing the elements apart

Pardon me, I am here too; as close as any one thing can be

Room for all greatness; we will work together and fit to a "Tee"

I can see stress, and acknowledge the many uncertainties in life

Allow me to extend the right hand of a spiritual fellowship and "Hope"

Hope is faith in what you believe to be true (lo que crees que es verdad)

One God; One Faith; One Baptism; the (Hope of new beginnings)

A great feeling of being here; let's participate together as life builds

Newness and spiritual gain; we have always been within, seen and unseen

It is now time for a change; pull from the deep, inner inspiration and pride

Write it loud; our pen will be heard, will be seen, somewhere and somehow

So let us now begin fully-equipped with all needs; and above all there is "Hope"

Mind Archeology

Nery Martinez, Jr.

Deep in the jungles of imagination,

Deep in layers of chiseled rocks

Where hidden pyramids,

Hidden artifacts,

Float

In a bubble

Under the surface

In the unknown

Unknown to oneself

Where no mirror casts a reflection,

Yet a reflection projects

Deep inside

As the eyes roll back

Deep at night

No longer hidden at the corners of the eyes

No longer blurred out of sight

Straight,

Look straight,

Stop

for a moment,

No more chisel,

The dust, brush out

Rediscover,

An ancient mural,

Handprints in the house

Early memories,

The first birthday, the smiles of dad, of mom,

the vibes of family, of love,

Painted the stucco canvas

What language couldn't describe

Here

As fresh paint,

Stuck in time

Blink,

Blink, blink,

A golden warrior shield reflects,

the times you couldn't overpower those nasty bullies,

so played the smart-ass boy to counter-fight

And told yourself a story of re-vindication before you could start to fly

Blink,

Blink, blink

The heavy jade ceremonial mask,

Precious on the outside but fails to show the man behind, that looks for validation instead of authenticity, let the mask rest under brave man

Blink,

Blink, blink

The crown of green quetzal feathers reveals,

How hard is to fight the wind and protect the nest with sticks,

The honor to be healthy and alive,

Yes as life as it is

Never underestimates the hidden treasures

One's mind

Sometimes

Fails to remind

Stop Worrying

Lois Jackson King

Please don't let the "woos" of what's going on get you down

With its challenges that make you want to wear a frown

Situation came like a storm; create an idea; a new possibility that's in you

Then, got use of internet; do the best that you know how to do

Put to work creative ideas, and do, which just may be a help to us all

We can be useful and be strengthened by each other's

strength, when working together in love and peace, doing which is right

Just stay focused, try keeping it tight

Don't let the "OOPS" of life keep you down

They are just bumps in the road, they are always around

Silent road blocks; called tricks of the enemy blocks; without making a sound

Hoping you lose focus with help of those so-called friends who let you down

Don't worry, make every effort to continue and move forward to higher ground

Those of real and true love will always be around

Delectable Collectables

Michelle Smith

I've never seen a U-Haul following a hearse
I've observed the opening of a wallet from a purse
Joyful fingers extracting a credit card
or cold hard cash
And to that indelible room her treasures
Near the window sill or corner
Those ceramics,
porcelain,
Or glass pieces
Space occupied
Her home is a retail museum
In colors of blue and white
On a clear day you can see forever
The sky and clouds
Are in view
A blue-earred bunny rabbit
A sphere with flowers and leaves
Fits in the palm of my hand
I'm reminded of that store called Bombay
My Nana's things
The grandchildren will remember
The stories and admiration on their faces

And each location

All were purchased from and their traces

Shared for future generations

A gleam in her eyes from her past to their present

We imagine her seeing these colors in heaven

Oh how Nana gleaned

Changes

Sanjuanita Martinez

I used to walk alone
looking for meaning,
Searching for answers,
Under the rocks;
In the fragrance of flowerbeds,
To no avail.

Then you came along.
Took my hand and dared me to dream.
You taught me life as we journeyed.
Soon after, along came our joys
With many tags attached.
Too many to mention.
But I still danced.
And you danced with me
To whatever melody came our way.

Until one day, it all crumbled.
I crumbled. Manual and all.
Uncertainty grasped my hand.
Suddenly,
Nothing made sense.

Again.

All is but a cloud,

not sure what type.

Day by day fades it away.

I am left with no answers.

The difference now:

It doesn't matter

At all…

Tick-Tock Clock of Life

Lois Jackson King

Have you heard the report that many people's lives are controlled by the hands of the clock? That is right; a man-made object taking control of when to do what it is you need to do, and how long it should take you to do it. My, my, they "Tick-Tock" their life away. Yes, the clock dictates to them.

Invisible power, but yet dictating in their life. We often hear statements such as "Time stands still for no man." "Time marches on."

How about "My head is spinning like a clock;" tell me, have you ever seen anyone's head spin? And here is a good one, "Time is too short to waste."

"With every tick of the clock, my heart beats just for you;" how crazy is that, what happens when and if the relationship stops, will his or her heart stop too?

The Book of Ecclesiastes 3:1-8, tells of time slots for the purpose of a certain thing, but there is no set or specific time in which to be governed by, and certainly not to be dictating.

We have freedom of choice. And there are some guidelines and rules to keep things (1 Corinthians 14:40) decent and in order; to balance and have self-discipline.

So let us govern ourselves to the "Ticking" of our own individual self as we stay connected to the source of all time slots, for all mankind; present and power unlimited, and none comparable "POWER."

Education, higher than the most highest of all intellectual minds, above the most brilliant and Noble Prize-winning Scientist in the world giving us, and at the same as given to us, "Time" to use our "Time" wisely and productively; in incorporating our gifts and talents to do magnificent things. So let us continue to timely proceed to the next level and reach our goal; "Together We Stand."

Always No

Tina Fallon

How does one go on?

Like an actor looking to be
noticed, the constant interviews
the constant emails, the applications.

The applications.

Why fight it? You push,
every day, you push
even in your dreams, trying
so hard to get ahead.
But the non-affirmative is back
in your face. You keep telling yourself
to believe in yourself. And yourself just keeps
on pushing. That is
not an answer that I can
accept, I can't
and I tell myself
I can. I can, I can
"Yes, you can!"

But years of the same, the same, "thank you no

thank you" from retail, unified school districts, charter schools,
sales and a plethora of management positions! So close,
so close to the full-

time, full-time but now you're just

a part-timer,

but I'd like to call it part-

part-time. Those positions to cover

your medical dental eyes.

Is it not in the cards

for me… I'm climbing

up the hill and *they* keep throwing

lava down. I get my hands

burned, they heal and I climb

again and again and

again. I'm tired

of climbing! I am losing

faith in society, in education and now

myself. When

does the reward happen,

when do I get the prize

and when

do I stop

this climb

Touch Down in Store

Lois Jackson King

Together we shall stand; you do you and I do me; different voices,
same purpose of reasoning

Let us together voice strongly: no chains, lynching, or biting dogs,

No broad offense, or injustice, can keep us from going forward

Together, we will stand. No silence, or standing in the back

We will be speaking, without shame. No, we don't need neon signs

We have no need for a marching band to announce our presence

Our voice will sound for us; making a choice, making a difference,
and giving an awakening

Giving aim to what is needed; making a stand for the concern
of self and the betterment of others

The march forward, we will be heard. We will speak out, against
every unfair and unconstitutional injustice that may prevail

There may be some battle wounds and disappointment

Many uncertainties we may have to face; but let us not fear.

Being a team player, we may be in some sense, on the front line

But interact as one; every word heard is a good position.

Be strong in what you believe; hold to it tight

We will not let go until it is time to pass it on.

As long as the goal is reached, our intention has been met

The most important fact is, we are doing it together

We can use our freedom of choice in all we say and do

Take pride in the value you bring as a team player

About the Authors
Sobre los autores

David Fallon

In the early 2000s, David Fallon published a handful of plays, poems, and stories. He took a 10 year sabbatical to build a career and raise a son. The recent death of his mother prompted him to return to writing—primarily short stories and an upcoming novel.

Ani Gohar Minasian

Ani Minasian is a Los Angeles-based Armenian-American writer of poetry, plays and songs in both Armenian and English. She earned her BA in Theatre Arts (playwriting emphasis) from Cal Poly Pomona, and has taught English and creative writing to grades 5–12. Her mind is a whirlwind of words, music and images, which she hopes to channel into projects that will bring a little more magic into the world, nurture emerging talent and creative peers, and promote tolerance and cultural understanding, especially of her Armenian culture.

Karyn Grasse

Karyn is a Monterey Park native and has been writing short stories and poems since she was 12. Sometimes, they get published. Sometimes, they sit in a box. Her most treasured creative endeavor, however, is the charming little person who has invaded her life for the past several years.

Luz Donis

Second generation Guatemalan, raised in Boyle Heights. Trained and worked as a nurse for L.A. County and L.A. Unified. Currently immersed in Vipassana meditation and Buddhist studies.

Lois Jackson King

Mother of 4 with 11 grandkids, 10 great grandkids. Her writings encourage and inspire, while some may have you laughing aloud.

Abraham Jaramillo

Abraham Jaramillo is a multimedia artist; illustrator, graphic designer, and photographer. His love for the arts began back when he created small sketch galleries for his grandmother when he was 8 years old. A longtime volunteer and teaching artist with DSTL Arts, Abraham enjoys and nurtures the pursuit of knowledge both in himself and others.

Mauricio Moreno (Soul on Fire)

Mauricio is an artist and writer, originally from the East Coast. He moved to California to fulfill his life mission of being a writer and sharing the stories of others to bring readers closer together and heal the world. He is currently working on a novel under the mentorship of Nicolás Obregón and is also in the process of publishing his first collection of poetry.

Gustavo Reyes Ramirez

Gustavo R. Ramirez is a poet-teacher-student-activist. He's excited to share his newly created mission statement: "I am a leader-servant—a worker among workers. My mission is to co-create peace, love, dignity, well-being, and fairness through leading by example and acting now. I will live life to the fullest with a sense of adventure and fun. I am committed to humble, bold, right action with integrity and courage."

Felicia Taylor E.

Felicia Taylor E. is a poet, writer, actress and arts educator. Her passion is in the Art of Healing. And she's facilitated writing and performing workshops at UCLA, California Museums, Pierce College and throughout LAUSD schools. Felicia has a BA in Journalism and Professional Certification in Theater from LAMDA. Baking and spending time with family is her fave time.

Kathy Vega

Kathy Vega resides in Atlanta, GA, but her birthplace is Los Angeles, California. Growing up in La Puente, CA, she has been influenced by her immigrant father and 1st-generation Mexican mother. She is grateful to be part of the Conchas workshop. It has freed her creative spirit!

Michelle Smith

Michelle Smith is a poet and artist working toward producing work that emits love and empathy for people of all kinds. She is a welcome addition to our Conchas y Café Zine family of artists.

Sanjuanita Martinez

Sanjuanita joins the Conchas y Café family from The Valley. A poet and educator, Sanjuanita writes from the heart, in the language that comes first, the language that best represents her voice.

Tina Fallon

Tina Fallon has contributed to *Conchas y Café* since 2015 and has published, *The Bin... and Other Pieces of Trash* in October of 2020. She has a BA in Theatre from Cal Poly Pomona and several courses in Elementary Education and Child Development. She loves avocados, piñas and tv!

Nery Martínez, Jr.

Nery Martínez, Jr. explores the edges of conflicting narratives, when one can barely speak, but surely write. Inspired by novels such as *Animal Farm*, *Persepolis*, and *Atlas Shrugged*, he grew disenchanted and curious at a young age. Nery loves to write about troubled worlds with his iPad and hammock, while floating in the middle of the trees, facing the waters of Lake Atitlán.

About the Conchas y Café program

Conchas y Café is a 12-week workshop series for adults, focusing exclusively on creative writing, literacy, and illustration. Participants have the opportunity to work with volunteer writers and artists on developing artwork that will be published and presented in a triannual 'zine and public reading.

For more information, locations, and dates for upcoming Conchas y Café workshops, contact us by email at *info@DSTLArts.org*.

Acerca el programa Conchas y Café

Conchas y Café es un taller de 12 semanas para adultos, especializando en escritura, literatura, y dibujo. Participantes tienen la oportunidad de trabajar con escritores y artistas voluntarios en el desarrollo de obras de arte que serán publicados y presentados en publicaciones trimestrales y lecturas públicas.

Para más información, localidades, y fechas de próximos talleres de Conchas y Café, contáctenos por correo electronico al *info@DSTLArts.org*.

This program is supported in part by:

CALIFORNIA ARTS COUNCIL

ART WORKS. | National Endowment for the Arts arts.gov

Los Angeles County Arts Commission

DCA DEPARTMENT OF CULTURAL AFFAIRS City of Los Angeles

DSTL arts

This publication was produced by DSTL Arts.

DSTL Arts is a nonprofit arts mentorship organization that inspires, teaches, and hires emerging artists from underserved communities.

To learn more about DSTL Arts, visit online at:

DSTLArts.org

@DSTLArts

/DSTLArts